Real Estate

Exact Blueprint on How to Grow Your Wealth

Real Estate Investing, Buying and Selling Homes & Property Management

Table of Contents

Introduction

Why Will I Get Into Real Estate Investing?

For many years, a lot of people who are into the path of real estate investing are often asking the question "How do I get into Real Estate Investing?" There are a lot of people in the United States, who would like to give real estate investing a try, are asking this question over and over again. Although a lot of them are trying to connect to investors through different blog posts, forums, articles, and different websites, there is still an indefinite question in their heads. There might be some books, articles, forums, and websites wherein you can see the answer and the answers they have might or might not work for everyone.

However, if you are looking for an easier way to get the answer, this is the book you are looking for. This guide will help you simplify the process of figuring out how you can get started. This guide is not ten thousand pages long and will guide you on every aspect of real estate investing. You will also get a broad overview of the best ways on how to get started and to gain financial freedom through real estate investments.

What Will You Expect In This Book?

There are six chapters in this book. Each chapter focuses on a specific part for your real estate investment journey. If you will be able to master them (which of course you will!), you can increase not only the money you will earn but also the chances of getting more and more real estate investments as well as minimizing the risk of failing or losing. This book will walk you through the following:

Knowing More about Real Estate Investing

Before you start investing in real estate, it is important that you know about the important concepts that it has. There are tons of different ways on how to get educated about real estate and how to build your knowledge base.

Choosing Your Real Estate Strategies and Specialties

You might be surprised but they're a lot of different strategies and approaches when it comes to the real estate business. The more you focus on one strategy and approach, the more knowledge you will get. This will be the main focus of Chapter 3, as we have to dig deeper and know what are the different niches, as well as the strategies you would need to undergo in order to gain profit from real estate investing.

Creating Your Real Estate Business Plan

In order for your real estate investing endeavors to be a success, you would need to create a strong foundation as well. You would need to create a more suitable business plan that will weather all the storms and struggles that you and your business will face. In Chapter 4, you will know what the best ways are when it comes to building a foundation for your real estate business.

Finding The Best Real Estate Properties

Since it is very important to find the best property to start on without paying too much for it, you will find the different criteria and decision-making strategies in Chapter 5.

Mastering the Real Estate Investment Market

Whether you are planning to invest in the city or in the countryside, you would need to focus not only in renting or selling out your properties but also in polishing your marketing skills. When it comes to the real estate business, it is not only having the right properties, marketing your properties is very important too.

Are You Ready To Start Your Real Estate Investing Journey?

Chapter 1: How to Invest In Real Estate – The Introduction

Are you new to the real estate investment business? A lot of people think that when it comes to learning how to invest in real estate properties, it is complicated, really difficult, and quite expensive. However, it is actually the other way around. In this chapter, you will learn how to start with real estate investment.

There are a lot of different investments where you can put your money – you can invest in stocks, in different bonds, mutual funds, currencies, and real estate. One of the most common reasons why a lot of people are investing in real estate is to gain financial freedom. However, before investing in real estate, it is very important that you, as well as your family, are 100% committed before deciding if you will move forward or not.

There are a lot of people who think that investing in real estate is like speculating or gambling. However, the truth is that there are a lot of ways on how to make money in real estate. There are some techniques that will require your full time while there are some which will only require a few hours of your time in a month. The amount of time you will spend in your investment depends on your approach, your strategy, your skills, your personality, your knowledge, and of course, your timeline. You don't need to make real estate your career if you do not want to. If you love your job and you do not want to quit it but still want to invest in real estate, then, you don't need to quit both. However, you can still get the better results if you are working as a full time real estate investor.

Investing In Real Estate Properties Even If You Have A Full Time Job?

Even if you are still keeping your day job, you can still take advantage of being a real estate investor. If you are investing on properties on the side, you do not need to live of any of the cash flow you are making from your 9 to 6 job. If you will be investing all the profits you are making from your real property investments onto another real estate property, you will be able to maximize the benefits of a more potential growth. You may partner in a larger piece of real estate property, buy and hold property or invest in mortgages. Real estate investing is a high profitable career.

Do You Need A Real Estate Investment Guru In Order For Your Investment To Be A Success?

Of course not! There are a lot of successful real estate investors who became successful without the help of paid investment gurus. There are a lot of real estate gurus who prey on people and possible investors who want to get rich faster and to get money easier. Often times, these gurus will tell you dangerous techniques and have you pay expensive courses, mentoring, and training. There are also some websites which will make you pay large referral fees and will guarantee you that you will get 50% of those fees in just a few days.

Can I Still Invest In Real Estate Even If I Have No Money At All?

Of course you can! It is possible to invest in real estate even if you do not have any money at all. However, also keep in mind that there is money involved in every real estate transactions. If you do not have your own money, you can still invest in real estate by using other people's money! Knowing how to invest in real estate without using your own money is considered as one of the most complex but important skill you would need to learn. If you cannot invest using your own money, you can bring someone on the table – all you just need is your intelligence, education, time, and creativity!

Chapter 2: Knowing More About Real Estate Investing

Without knowledge, expertise, and preparation about real estate investing, you might either disappoint yourself for making bad decisions or you may also trash your real estate opportunities and dealings. This part is very important in your real estate investing career because you will know all the sources where you will get the information about real estate investing.

Do Not Start Without Equipping Yourself.

Unlike what others think it is, investing in real estate is not a fast source of easy money. Same with constructing a building or even a simple house, you would need to know how to build the foundation. By knowing how the foundation is made, it will help you know how to build the building.

There are wide ranges of approaches to get instructed in real estate investment. You don't even have to pay hundreds or a huge number of dollars to take into the business. In this part, you will discover some sources of real estate investing education. Make sure to consider each before settling on an official choice on how you're going to get up and get started. Also, remember that what works for other people may not work for you. So, you have to do your own research and come up with strategies that suit only you. Do not over rely on anyone or anything and remember that you are your only and best source to not just get started in real estate but also move forward in the right direction. As and when you start buying and selling houses, you will know to continue with it and reach a stage where you absolutely need no help doing it. In fact, you can surpass that stage and turn into a mentor to others interested in doing the same in property investments.

Sources of Real Estate Investing Education

Books

Books are considered as the best sources of learning for most real estate investors – they are important in getting knowledge about real estate investing – what the different theories and techniques about it are, as well as the do's and don'ts. Different bookstores and authors that contain knowledge about real estate produce not only hundreds but also thousands of real estate books yearly. If you are looking for ways on how to get more money in real estate investing, there is definitely a book where you can find that information. However, if you do not like reading books or spending time sitting by a corner, you have other choices. Why don't you try and search for eBooks instead? With eBooks, you can read them anytime and anywhere you are! Why don't you also give audio books a try? Why are audio books recommended especially for busy people? Think of it as someone reading the book to you. You do not need to turn to different pages anymore simply because there's a voice over for you already! Remember to pick reliable books though and ensure that the authors are experts in the subject matter. You must try to look at the material through various angles and ensure that you have thoroughly understood the subject. If you are finding it difficult to find good books then ask around for advice on the best books that are available in the market. Maybe they will point you to certain gems that will not only help you get started in the business of real estate but also increase your overall confidence in it.

Blogs

If you are not familiar with blogs, it is either you do not have access to the Internet or you just simply do not like the idea of Internet browsing. Blogs are very popular now. There are a lot of people who have their own blog pages, which they use to talk about either a certain topic or different topics about a lot of things. Similar with books, you can get a lot of information from blogs! There are a lot of people nowadays who are into making and maintaining their own blogs, so you have a lot of sources to choose from! There are a lot of great posts written by different people who are investing in real estate. What you just need to do is to search for them, read their posts, and learn from all their writings. If you don't know where to look then simply type in the words real estate blogs and a slew of posts will appear. You have to choose the best ones from amongst them and start reading as much as you can. Once you understand how all of it works, not only will you be able to find more blogs on the Internet, but also start writing your own! You will see that it is quite easy to access it and cost much lesser than what books on the subject matter would cost you.

Mentors

Mentors are considered as the most powerful, the easiest, and the most used way in order to gain information about real estate. There are a lot of professional real estate mentors who you can talk with. Some of them will charge you for their services – however, there are also a lot of mentors who will just charge you with the same price as a coffee shop charges for a cup of coffee. You will surely learn a lot from them since they are real estate investors too. There are a lot of people who would like to share what they know and successful real estate investors are one of them. All you just need to do is to introduce yourself to one of your local real estate investor. Keep in mind that the more people you know, the more opportunity that you will learn about the field. Here too, you have to find reliable sources for yourself. Just ensure that you are looking at all the right places for the information as the knowledge that you gain from it is of vital importance. Don't be quick to judge someone, as they might not be what they appear to be. Someone who looks quite knowledgeable might end up supplying you with mediocre knowledge and someone that looks disinterested might give away vital information. So don't be too quick to judge someone. They will only be able to help you to the extent that you allow them to and cannot do so beyond that.

Podcasts

Podcasting is considered as one of the greatest innovations not only for social media and learning but also for real estate education. What is podcasting or podcast? A podcast is a recorded audio program. Think of a radio show that is produced by using a simple computer and a microphone.

There are a lot of great podcasts. By using your smart phone, your car stereo, your computer or your MP3 player, you can download and listen to them any-where and anytime you want – whether you are in bed, you are exercising in the gym, jogging or in your car. And the best part, it is actually for FREE! If you are not tech savvy then don't worry, you can avail the help of someone and get them to get you started on it. Don't assume things and simply start with it. You will see how easy and useful it really is to use podcasts and will decide to abandon your old methods for it. With time, you will start podcasting yourself and thereby increase self-knowledge on the subject. Remember, there is nothing like too much information and the more you learn the better. Consider yourself a sponge that can absorb information and know when and how to use it.

You Don't Need To Be A Genius!

If you want to invest in a real estate property, you do not need to be a MBA holder or a college degree holder in order for you to understand the real estate math. Well in fact, the math that you will be doing with real estate investment is actually grade school level math. So don't worry about your qualification, as it will not matter here. It is the same as how you don't need to be a commerce graduate to invest in stocks. All you have to do is understand the basics, know what to do and when and you are all set to take on the real estate business by the horns. This book will serve as your one true real estate guide and usher you into the right direction. If at any point in time you do get confused, then simply open up this book and have your issues resolved.

Income
The amount of money that you will be getting from your real estate property is your income. Computing for your income is the easiest math that you will do. You just need to simply add the amount of rent you will be charging as well as the additional fees along with it. For example, you own a one-door rental apartment. The apartment rent is

$750 and the tenant is paying you additional $20 for garage use. Your total income will be $770. Now multiply it by 12 and you have your yearly income, multiplied by 6 will give you your half yearly income etc. Apart from this, you can also do the simple calculation of seeing how much profit you are left with after you have sold your old house and bought a new one. All you have to do is look at your selling amount and the cost of the new house and subtract the two. You will be left with the profit amount that you have earned. All of this is simple math and nothing complicated about it.

Expenses

Expenses are the amount that will cost you from maintaining your investment. For example, the building fee for your apartment is $50 a month. You would also need to pay the garbage fee of $50. Add in the maintenance fee of $100 a month. The total amount of your expense is $200. There might be other expenses that as a real estate investor like you would need to pay such as insurance, taxes, association fee, and other fees that the neighborhood or the government will require you to pay. There will be many other expenses that will come up. You have to maintain a journal and make a note of all the different expenses. Don't make the mistake of making just a mental note of them, you will get confused. You have to jot it down immediately and not take it casually. If you don't have the habit, then it is important that you develop it at the earliest. If you have a partner, then ask them to remind you or they make a note of it themselves.

Cash Flow

The amount of money that will be left at the end after all the expenses are deducted will be your cash flow. To know it, you just need to get the difference between the income and the total amount of expenses. By using the examples above, the total cash flow you will be getting is $570 a month. Not bad for a starter, right? You will realize that this number consistently goes up and you will have the chance to make a lot of money. Again, it is important that you maintain a record of it. Don't make the mistake of taking this step lightly. You have to ensure that you are making a record of everything and are doing your best to avoid any mistakes in the calculations. Every penny counts and you have to account for all the money that you come into.

Return on Investment

Return on Investment, which is more popularly known as ROI, is the annual interest rate that you will be getting from your real estate property. For example, if you invested $500 on your property and you earned $500 from that property investment, which will make a total of $1000, you made a 100% return on your investment.

If you invested $2500 on a studio apartment and you made $5000 investment over a course of one year, you just made a whooping 200% investment for yourself! To know how much your return of investment is, you may get it by getting the difference between your total balance and the balance you have when you started.

You have to understand that you might not always be lucky enough to get such a large return on investment. You have to try and maximize it as much as possible. One big mistake that most people make is not anticipating a good rate of return. You have to remain confident and ensure that you know exactly how much you will get from your investment.

Getting A Real Estate Mentor

For cases or situations wherein you are more comfortable with someone doing all the work for you or someone who will be supplying all the information without the need of reading the books and instructions or computing your cash flow, you can get a real estate mentor instead.

Focuses first on knowing whom the real state mentors near your place are. If there's no one near you, you may need to research and find them. The guide you would need should be able to teach you how to possess more stable real estate properties and how you can use it as a full time work. The key is discovering a person that you need to gain from in the field you need to enter. While you can gather a ton of data from any effective financial specialist, it is important to find a mentor who knows how to gain profit from an average studio apartment up to a large commercial building. Search out people who are doing what you need to do.

It is important for you to look for someone genuine, who will be capable of helping you in the best possible manner. It will pay to not only do some research but also look at the different testimonials that have been left behind for the person. These will give you a good idea of whether the mentor is a good one or not. Once you get your hands on the right mentor, you must establish a good rapport with him. Your camaraderie will matter, as the two of you will need to work closely in order for you to find the right house or property for yourself. If the two of you are not on the same page then you will end up making mistakes in terms of buying your property.

It is also important that others will see you as a significant person, especially when you are seeking for a mentor. Think of the things that you will be able to offer a person if you want to seek or get their help. Can you offer your services for free if they need to fix something? Maybe you have superb web hosting abilities or can you build an advertising website for him? Make it your objective to give strong worth to each relationship that you have. Keep in mind that you don't fundamentally need to do everything for nothing for that individual. In the event that you are helpful – maybe simply being a reliable support individual who doesn't scam them is sufficient to construct that relationship. Continuously think a win-win situation. Don't just concentrate on what's in it for you.

How to Overcome Your Fear of Real Estate Education

Although there are a lot of successful real estate investors out there, there are also handfuls that are excessively loaded with apprehension and vulnerability, making it impossible for them to ever really do an arrangement. In the event that you are simply starting, odds are that you have some fears too. However don't stress yourself – fear is a characteristic piece of life and is intended to help us maintain a strategic distance from terrible choices and the outcomes got there from. So don't blame your fear unnecessary and learn to combat it. Overcoming your fear can also help you to start from the beginning. You will eventually discover yourself not wasting your time. As long as you are going about it the right way, you have the chance to overcome anything that you set your mind to. In this segment, we will look at the things that you can do to overcome your fear of property.

Get off Your Fear.

Whether you are looking for joining the real estate investment business because you want to use your spare time and money or you would like to leave your stressful day job, you cannot start if you are having doubts or fears. You will obviously assume that your fears are right and that you are better off without taking on unnecessary investments. But in reality, it is best to combat this fear at the earliest as you might end up losing out on a lot of lucrative deals. Don't think it will affect you negatively as that is only a misconception. You can easily make a career out of it and create an alternate source of income for yourself. Through the course of this book, you will find it increasingly easy to invest in real estate and have fruitful returns.

You should start building up an arrangement and work that arrangement regularly. It is as simple as getting up, going to work, and receiving your paycheck regularly. A fruitful real estate investor may have some down situation but all you just need to do is to wake up, to restart, and to believe that you can do it. Working for your own self is fruitful – it is a career and a gift at the same time.

Stop buying costly courses or materials. Instead, seek you mentors or coaches.

In the event that you are not dedicated, there will be no course, class or mentor whom going to get you any closer to your objective. Every real estate course out there spotlights on the mechanics. However, the genuine activity and your own motivation are those that will give you success. When you can get that under control - it won't make any difference even if whatever procedure you utilize. You will never discover accomplishment as a real estate investor!

Keep in mind that you could spend a considerable amount of cash having somebody to demonstrate the mechanics. However, in the event that you are not eager to manage the "molding" issue, you are simply squandering cash.

Learn the language of real estate investors.

Once you build up your confidence in understanding the lingo, your ability to start a conversation with others while understand the discussion will grow exponentially.

Watch others and involve yourself in other investors and activities.

On the off chance that this implies pulling all-nighters and weekends for a nearby speculator for nothing, then that is the cost of affirmation. You will rapidly figure out how to beat your apprehension when you help other people fulfill achievement, giving you the certainty to strike out naturally. All ventures have some level of danger and real estate investing is no special case. While hazard can't be kept away from, it can be overseen through legitimate readiness – a skill that you will surely learn over time. The hardest thing to do in any new pursuit is to begin.

Chapter 3: Choosing Your Real Estate Strategies And Specialties

Although at first it may appear that the most important part of real estate investing is to know the most about it, in reality, it is just concentrated in two things: (1) to know what exactly the business is; and (2) to know what are the strategies and techniques to get into the business. This section is going to acquaint you with the absolute and most prevalent strategies. Additionally, you will also know what are the most widely recognized procedures for pushing ahead.

Real Estate Investments Are Like Choosing The Best Shoes In A Store

Have you ever experienced going into a shoe store and having difficulties picking out the best pair of shoes for yourself? You may surely spent too much time thinking which is the best one to get but at the same time, the pair which will not leave you saying "I wasted my money for nothing". It is the same as real estate investing. Knowing where to put your money is the same as knowing where to spend your cash onto those shoes.

There are handfuls, if not hundreds, of distinctive approaches to profit as a real estate investor. It depends upon you to pick the corner you need to get into. You may totally choose and follow a few specialties and methods since there might be some strategies that will now work for you. Keep in mind that in choosing the strategy to follow,

16

you should choose the ones that you think will work best. Best of all, you don't have to pick every one of them. Figuring out how to effectively put these resources into reality and turning yourself into an expert is the most important.

This part is going to open up those many shoes for you to test. You will see probably the most widely recognized ones up to least used ones. Remember that once you know the techniques you need to begin with, you should work on it until the very end. By turning into a real estate investor and specialist, you can start building your own real estate properties and empire.

Choosing Your Real Estate Investment Niche

There are a lot of real estate niches, as well as well known kinds of properties that you can choose from once you started investing in real estate properties. Each one of these real estate investment niches has their own subsets. This is just a rundown of the most popular real estate properties that you can begin with.

Single-Family Homes
Maybe the most widely recognized property for most first time real estate investors is the single family home. Single-family homes are generally simple to lease, simple to offer, and simple to fund. That being said, in numerous states, the rents investors get from single-family rentals may not be sufficient to give positive income. Also there is the danger of losing out on 100% income if nobody is interested in taking the house. That is a big risk and you

must not overlook it. It is best to invest in a single-family home along with other types of investments if you wish to avoid any loss.

Duplex / Triplex / Quads

Little multifamily properties, which are usually two to four units, are joined together for the advantage of a growing family. These properties can be purchased legitimately. A real estate investor can get income from these properties entirely well and there is frequently less rivalry and competition than what you will experience if you will be offering single-family homes. Best of all, these properties can serve as a strong foundation of your real estate investment career. Another advantage of the little multifamily property is the capacity to exploit "economies of scale" as you can secure not only 1 but also 2 or up to 4 units in a single transaction. One of the things that make these speculations so engaging is that most banks take a gander at little multifamily properties with four units or less with the same rules as a solitary family house, which can make meeting all requirements for an advance much simpler.

Small Apartments

Little flat structures are comprised of somewhere around five to fifty units. In spite of the fact that the line in the middle of little and expensive lofts is not an unavoidable reality, most real estate investors normally lay down a meaningful boundary in the middle of little and substantial condo structures at around 50 units. These properties can be harder to purchase than single family homes or 2 to 4 unit properties, as they depend on business loaning norms rather than private ones. However, these properties regularly give noteworthy income to the real estate investor that can manage the more administration exceptional nature of the properties.

Also, competition with other real estate investors for these kinds of properties is relatively low for it is too expensive to purchase these properties, giving more profit to the investor who owns it.

Large Apartments

This class of property, the large Apartments, are the large complexes you might see all across the country that often include pools, work-out rooms, full time staff, and high advertising budgets. These properties can cost many millions of dollars to purchase but can produce stable returns with minimal personal involvement. They are better known as gated communities or apartment complexes. If you wish to buy something like this then you should be ready to shell out a lot of money. Before you do so, check if you have the resources for it. Don't make the mistake of committing to a property without understanding your own limit. You will end up with a huge debt, which will wreak havoc in your life. Check if you are able to afford something of the sort and only then invest in it. Many large apartments are owned by organizations that are small groups of investors who pool their resources.

Commercial

Commercial investments can vary dramatically in sizes, styles, and purpose but ultimately involve a property that is leased to a business. Some commercial investors rent buildings to small local businesses while others rent large spaces to supermarkets or big box megastores. While commercial properties often provide good cash flow and consistent payments, they also may carry with them much longer holding periods during times of vacancies. A commercial property can often sit empty for many months or years. Unless you are starting from a very solid financial position, investing in commercial real estate is not recommended for beginners. We will look at these types in detail a little later in this book.

Choose Your Real Estate Investing Strategies

The segment above took a gander at various distinctive venture vehicles that you can use to put resources into investments. Then again, when figuring out how to put resources into investments, it is insufficient to just about what these property specialties are. Rather, as a real estate investor, you would need to utilize a mixed bag of systems when managing these ventures to deliver income to your pocket. There are two most well known techniques that you can use to profit with these investments.

Wholesaling

Wholesaling is the procedure of discovering extraordinary land arrangements, making an agreement to secure the arrangement, and after that, offering the agreement to another purchaser. Most of the time, a wholesaler never really claims the property they are searching and offering; rather, a wholesaler essentially discovers extraordinary arrangements utilizing an assortment of promoting methods, puts them under contract, and offers that agreement to another for a "task charge." This expense is regularly in the middle of $500 and $5,000 all things considered or all the more relying upon the measure of the arrangement. Basically, the wholesaler is an agent who is paid for discovering arrangements.

A few wholesalers offer their agreement to retail purchasers. However, most offer their agreement to different speculators (frequently house flippers) who are commonly "money purchasers." When managing these money purchasers, a wholesaler can regularly get paid for the number of days or weeks they work.

Numerous real estate investors decide to choose wholesaling because of its notoriety of being a simple technique and it is considered as one with the low-start up expenses when first starting. Since the property is never really possessed by the wholesaler, there are no recovery expenses, advance charges, foremen, inhabitants, banks, or different muddling's. Wholesaling is the most famous technique taught by real estate property masters and frequently gets the most consideration therefore. However, it is not as simple to turn into an effective wholesaler as they make it sound.

Wholesalers should consistently search out for the best arrangements with a specific end goal to have stock to offer to others and must have a very much-outlined promoting channel to ceaselessly pull in these leads. Wholesalers additionally should ceaselessly search out purchasers for the arrangements they gain. While advanced as a methodology that anybody can do, even somebody with ZERO cash, you would need to have the best sources and the best marketing skills to move forward. Having said that, the individuals who hold on in developing their wholesaling aptitudes regularly discover extraordinary achievement and a decent wellspring of wage while they develop their insight into other, more beneficial methods.

Buy and Hold

Maybe the most widely recognized type of contributing is the "purchase and hold procedure". The buy and hold procedure includes obtaining a property and leasing it out for an expanded duration of time. It's presumably the most straightforward and purest type of real estate investment procedure that there is. Basically, a "Purchase and Hold" investor looks to make riches by leasing the property out and either gathering month to month income or just holding the property until it can be sold for an larger amount later on. Amongst the benefits of this system is that amid the time that you hold the property and rent it out, the home loan is paid down every single month, diminishing your main adjust and expanding your value in the property.

Standouts amongst the most vital things for another purchase and hold investor to comprehend is the manner by which to assess arrangements and opportunities. The most well known slip-up that we see new real estate property investors make with this system is purchasing terrible arrangements in light of the fact that they essentially don't comprehend property assessment. Other normal issues incorporate thinking little of costs, settling on terrible choices on occupant determination, and neglecting to oversee appropriately. These slip-ups can all be kept away from, in any case, on the off chance that you basically take in the business. Bouncing in without fitting training can be to a great degree excessive both fiscally and once in a while, lawfully.

To appropriately do the Buy and Hold method, a real estate investor ought to figure out how to legitimately distinguish the back and forth movements of the business sector that a property is situated in. Eventually, when they see the business sector and the properties they are keen on to be at a low point, wherein the cost is low and the tax is high, the purchase and hold property investor will try to buy properties. At the point, when the business sector gets to be over-warmed, an accomplished Buy & Hold investor will normally quit purchasing until they see things settle down. Amid these moderate periods, they may offer or essentially keep on holding their properties. There are a lot of Buy & Hold investors who never offer a property, picking rather to pay the home loan off and live on the income or may at last offer utilizing "Merchant Financing".

Chapter 4: Creating Your Real Estate Business Plan

No awesome building is made without watchful arranging before the ground is broken. This arrangement serves as the guide for the advancement of the structure, since without this the building just won't meet up. In the same way, precisely making your real estate strategy for success is a necessary piece of your trip. This part will concentrate on the choices you have in building that arrangement and will set you up for your passage and long haul accomplishment, in real estate investment.

Making a Real Estate Investing Business Plan

If you somehow happened to get in your car and take a street trip from your place over to a territory you have never bee, would you simply believe your gut and begin going in the general course you need to get to? No doubt, you will surely bring with a guide or your advanced mobile phone's GPS.

The reason we utilize guides is on the grounds that generally the street is capricious and the right street may appear to prompt the wrong place. Different times the wrong street may appear to indicate specifically your destination. Guides are made to demonstrate the least demanding course, the pitfalls you need to evade, and unique things to see along the way. The same guideline applies for your excursion into real estate investment. This area you are going to examine will build the guide that you'll take after on your voyage. Most popularly, we call it the "strategy to success".

What Your Real Estate Business Plan Should Include

Statement of purpose
At the point when individuals ask you what you do, what do you let them know? This is statement of purpose ought to plainly characterize your motivation and ought to incorporate the advantages your business gives. Do your exploration and concoct a strong statement of purpose. This is the "why" in your street trip.

Objectives
Where would you like to go? What do you need land to help you to accomplish? In the event that your objective is to make $5,000 every month in automated revenue, record that. In the event that your objective is to flip four homes for every month, record that as well. These objectives may change after some time, influencing whatever is left of your strategy for success – and that is all right. Make it to a point to put down both short and long haul objectives. By setting littler, more achievable objectives, you will give yourself something to dependably anticipate finishing. This will help you stay.

Strategy
There are several approaches to profit in land – yet you needn't bother with hundreds. You essentially need to pick one system and turn into an expert of it. That methodology or vehicle, if reliable, will bring you through to your destination and objectives. On the off chance that you are deciding to flip homes to produce trade out request to set

aside enough to leave your place of employment, record that. On the off chance that you are hoping to fabricate easy revenue from little multifamily properties for your retirement, record that. Try not to stress in the event that you don't comprehend or know how you're going to achieve everything in the arrangement. Keep in mind that your marketable strategy can and will change in time, and as you learn, you'll round the arrangement out with more points of interest.

Time allotment
What is your time allotment to achieve your objectives? Be practical. However, don't be hesitant to reach either. Would you like to resign in ten years? Is it true that you are anticipating in leaving your place of employment one month from now? Report your timetable here. You can do this as per your objectives, as said.

Market
Characterize your business sector. What sort of property will you be searching for, low salary, high income, or business zones? As a tenderfoot – pick a zone you feel most good with. Most new investors ought to anticipate contributing inside of a short driving separation to your home, as opposed to contributing long separation, unless your area makes it incomprehensible, doing this will help you to turn into a real estate investment specialist, which will help you all the more effortlessly break down arrangements and opportunities. It will likewise help you know the players in the zone, which will at last help you discover accomplices, and again opportunities.

Criteria
Before you go out and begin searching for gives, you have to build up the criteria that those arrangements must fall

in. You'll need to characterize your credit to esteem, income necessities, max buy sum, max recovery sum, max time allotment, and so forth. These are all things you'll get as we go further. A standout amongst the most critical lessons you can learn is to adhere to your criteria, leave any arrangement that does not meet your criteria. It is anything but difficult to end up candidly appended to an arrangement. However, by adhering to your criteria, you take the feeling good and take out those that are not. On the off chance that you are not sufficiently discovering arrangements to single out from, you can change your business and/or procedure. You'll take in more about these zones of criteria. This some piece of your strategy for success is a standout amongst the most critical to completely comprehend and unmistakably characterize. An excess of new real estate investors get energized and purchase the first arrangement that comes to their direction. By having unmistakably characterized criteria, you have the capacity to effortlessly dismiss the 99% of properties that are not a decent arrangement.

Chapter 5: Finding The Best Real Estate Properties

So far, we have concentrated on the planning required before contributing. On the other hand, as we've talked about before in this guide, it's insufficient essentially to examine bargains. Sooner or later, you should take the dive and purchase your first property. This part is going to concentrate on the most ideal approaches to locate the best properties, arrange the best arrangement, and verify you overcome shutting in one piece.

The Most Effective Method to Profit When You Buy Your Investment Property

As the well-known land cited toward the beginning of this section states, you should make your benefit when you purchase. In many cases, you won't begin your contributing vocation via finding a gigantic check; these checks come after you effectively execute your venture techniques. The benefits you make, in any case, can be made or wrecked at the season of procurement. So what does it intend to "benefit when you purchase?"

To make your benefit when you purchase, you must buy a property at a value that guarantees you make your fancied benefits, based upon your capacity to execute your way out method. At the end of the day, you have to purchase savvy. In the event that you unfathomably overpay for a property, no measure of wishing, trusting or change is going to make your venture advantageous. While you can't foresee with

100% exactness, where the business is going to go, you can know where it's at today.

123 Pitt Street is right now recorded at $300,000, and late tantamount deals demonstrate that the comparable homes have sold for in the middle of $280,000 and $290,000. 123 Pitt Street, be that as it may, needs about $50,000 worth of work to be in pleasant condition. Hence, in the event that you pay $280,000 for it and put in $50,000 - you'll be at $170,000 and that doesn't number all the end expenses, holding expenses, offering expenses, unexpected overages, or different charges that you'll need to pay. You will be submerged (owe more than it's worth) on this property regardless of the amount of work you do to it. On the other hand, if comparative homes were esteemed at $225,000, you would find that you had, to be sure, made your benefit when you purchased.

The same standard applies to rental venture properties. In the event that all your month to month costs (counting assessments and protection) on 123 Pitt Street was $1500 every month and the normal rent got every month was $1000 every month - you will be losing cash every month. Nonetheless, if normal rents were $3,000 every month and your aggregate costs were just $1000 - you would be gainful from the day you purchased it.

It's regularly said by experienced financial specialists that income is the "what tops off an already good thing." You make your benefit when you purchase when you buy a property in view of what it would be worth today, not what it may be worth sometime in the future. In the event that a speculation looks bad without income, don't put resources into it. This is known as "conjecturing" and, while it might be gainful for some, is an unsafe endeavor for both unpracticed and experienced real estate investors alike.

Criteria When Purchasing A Real Estate Property

Since you comprehend why getting an awesome arrangement is essential (to secure your benefits toward the starting), it is now the opportunity to begin searching for a property. Before, you do you have to characterize your choice criteria. This segment will concentrate on what your criteria is, the reason it makes a difference, and how to characterize it.

Envision that you need to utilize another formula in making your dinner today. You take out a cookbook to discover a recipe that looks great, find an awesome prepared chicken feast, and make your shopping rundown of fixings to make the supper for your family. You make a beeline for the store and start grabbing the things on your rundown. Chicken, basil, olive oil, and different things start to fill your cart. All of a sudden, you see the spaghetti and recollect another recipe that you once needed to attempt with spaghetti. You start to go after the spaghetti then recollects your shopping rundown. Spaghetti isn't on the rundown for this evening's supper, so you set back the diversion and proceed on your path home to make an impeccable supper for your crew.

Real Estate is the same. Your choice criteria rundown is much the same as your fixing rundown in the case above. It is intended to keep you concentrated on looking for the things you require and not squander cash on other attractive things along the way. Real Estate is an energizing field with a variety of specialties and procedures so it is anything but difficult to get occupied by the other enormous properties. Having unmistakably characterized choice criteria can help you stay centered, maintain a strategic distance from "examination loss of motion", and keep you on track to purchase an incredible venture property. By characterizing your criteria, you will have the capacity to restrict down the decisions in the business, and you will then dispose of the lion's share of arrangements that are just diversions. Rather, you'll concentrate on discovering only the sort of arrangements that you are occupied with purchasing.

There are various distinctive things you will need to consider to add to your "criteria list." These could include:

- Location
- Size of the property
- Size of the property's lot
- Condition of the property
- Cash flow
- Appreciation Potential

Nobody can let you know precisely what your venture property criteria ought to or ought to exclude. Some of it will boil down to individual inclination, for example, "I just need to purchase in Seattle" or "I just need houses with storm cellars". However, the greater part of your picked criteria will spin around the sort of speculation you are getting into. For instance, in the event that you are hoping to turn into a "purchase and hold" specialist of little multifamily units, your criterion is going to incorporate little multifamily properties and will reject old business structures.

By indicating early, what criteria you are willing to take a gander at, your pursuit turns out to be substantially more sensible. In the same way, you have the capacity to more successfully impart your longings to other people who may help you purchase property. In the event that you basically told individuals "I am searching for land," then no doubt reaction would be "useful for you..." However, in the event that you rather said that you were looking "to purchase a little single family house in the Los Angeles neighborhood for under $150,000" you empower others to consider properties that may coordinate that depiction and get you joined with the arrangement.

Rules of Investing In Real Estate Properties

Maybe the most essential piece of the criteria you set up together is the money related segment. On the off chance that an arrangement doesn't bode well monetarily, it's not going to be an in number speculation for you. In section two we took a gander at a percentage of the essential math encompassing land contributing, for example, wage, income, and rate of profitability. As a rule, a posting is not going to let you know the vital data you need to think about the financials of a property. Yes, you can for the most part focus the measure of salary the property makes – however, you won't know promptly the amount of month to month income the property produces, how overrated the property is or what you ought to offer. Moreover, it's not going to bode well to get out your spreadsheet and do a full property assessment on each and every arrangement you look at. This is when the guidelines become possibly the most important factor.

A standard is another way to say general guideline. Rules can help give you a speedy approach to assess a property's financials on the fly. Similarly as with any general guideline, utilizing tenets is not a definite science and ought to never depend on completely to choose if a property is a decent venture. However, they can help you rapidly channel a property and choose in the event that it's worth further assessment. We should examine a couple of these standards:

The 2% standard expresses that your month-to-month rent ought to be more or less 2% of the price tag. At the end of the day, a $50,000 home ought to lease for $1,000 every month; a $150,000 home ought to lease for $2,000 every month. This is an exceptionally traditionalist gauge that is extremely oversimplified but can help in choosing if a property warrants a more profound look. In many parts of the nation, the 2% is extremely hard to accomplish, yet the closer you can get to that, the better income you'll get.

An average studio apartment rents for $1000 per month in your neighborhood. According to the 2% rule - you should be looking to spend around $50,000 for that property ($1000 / .02 = $50,000)

The 2% is an extraordinary general guideline that helps you to reasonably precisely anticipate how much your costs are going to cost you every month for a property. The

2% basically expresses that half of your salary will be spent on costs, excluding the home loan installment. As specified above, most land postings will tell you what the month-to-month pay of a property is. By partitioning that number down the middle, you have the capacity to effectively perceive the amount you'll have left to pay the month-to-month contract. Any wage left over, after the half of costs and the home loan installment are taken out, is your income. The half of costs incorporates all costs, including repairs, opening, utilities, charges, protection, administration, turnover costs, and the periodic first class repairs that must be set something aside from other capital expenses such as rooftops, parking areas, and heaters.

A loft building gets $10,000 every month in salary. Utilizing the 2%, we are left with $5,000 to make the home loan installment. On the off chance that the month-to-month contract installment on the property was $4,500 every month, you can sensibly accept a month-to-month income of $500 every month.

The 2% is particularly useful in showing that costs are quite often more than one might suspect. One basic slip-up that new real estate investors make is under-assessing how much the costs are going to cost. The 2% serves to demonstrate that there are dependably costs that are surprising, so get ready for them.

The 70% standard is utilized by speculators to rapidly focus the most extreme value one ought to pay for a property taking into account the after repair esteem. In spite of the fact that frequently utilized by house flippers, the 70% tenet can really be utilized for any procedure when you need to locate a decent arrangement. The 70% standard says that you ought to just pay 70% of what the after repair quality is, less the repair costs.

Keep in mind that a general guideline like the ones above are utilized just to rapidly and productively screen a property and choose on the off chance that it's worth further examination. Never utilize a general guideline to choose precisely the amount to pay or on the off chance that you ought to contribute or not. In the event that a property passes the above standards or draws near, it might be justified regardless of a more definite investigation on paper or through a PC spreadsheet. Try not to confound a general guideline for a permit to skip getting your work done.

Process of Buying A Real Estate Property

When you purchase a property, you don't just compose a check to the vendor and get the keys. The procedure of purchasing and offering land is a complex and regularly long wander that has numerous moving parts. This area is going to walk you through the progressions, from start to finish.

Step One: You choose your venture method or specialty.

Step Two: You characterize your choice criteria.

Step Three: You choose the strategy for financing the arrangement. This implies that you will have a reasonable arrangement of how you are going to buy the property. In the event that you are anticipating utilizing a bank advance, you will need to be pre-endorsed. If you anticipate, rather, utilizing all your money, you will need to have that cash fluid and prepared to be utilized.

Step Four: You start looking on the MLS or business inquiry destinations like Loopnet.com, the daily paper classifieds, standard mail, yard signs, and every other road to discover properties available to be purchased. You presumably will unite with a land operator too, as they are by and large free for the purchaser. These land operators are normally paid out of the vendor's end costs. In the event that you are managing specifically with homes that are not recorded on the MLS, you most likely won't utilize a land operator; you would simply contact the vendors themselves.

Step Five: You run every property through a rundown of criteria channels to immediately screen out the duds. These channels are in light of the criteria you set and in addition, the guidelines we examined before in this part.

Step Six: You make an offer on the property (or properties) that you need to seek after. You may offer not exactly what you are really ready to spend or you may offer your primary concern. Ordinarily, an offer is made utilizing a "Buy and Sale Agreement" which your real estate specialists will undoubtedly accomplish for you. On the off chance that you are not purchasing a property from the MLS and don't utilize a specialist, you can normally get a fill-in-the-clear buy and deal assertion on the web, at a paper supply store, from a lawyer or free from a nearby Title and Escrow organization.

Step Seven: You arrange the arrangement with the merchant and provided that this is true, gone to a commonly acknowledged concurrence on value and terms.

Step Eight: You perform your further examine the property. The property points of interest are then given over to either a Title or Escrow organization or a nearby lawyer (contingent upon your State). Amid this time, you will likewise submit the required printed material for your financing. You'll start coating up foremen. If work is required, you'll keep an eye on the legitimacy of the financials given about the property, and you'll get ready for shutting in taking care of whatever different issues or issues come up. This procedure can take anyplace from a few days to a while or more, relying upon the circumstance. Bank financing is for the most part the reason this procedure takes longer, so in the event that you are utilizing all money, closings can be much snappier.

Step Nine: You sign papers at the Title and Escrow or lawyer's office. Soon thereafter (or just after a few days, depending on your area) all the papers will be recorded, and you'll be the new proprietor.

Chapter 6: Mastering The Real Estate Investment Market

Regardless of what kind real estate property investment you decided to participate in, you will most likely need to utilize your advertisement and marketing skills. Advertising is the procedure of offering your services and real estate properties to other people to drive your business forward. Where you take your business is completely subject to you and your promoting skills.

As a real estate investor, the first and most essential thing you'll be advertising is yourself – your own particular individual brand. It doesn't take a considerable measure of cash, and it doesn't take a great deal of time. You will start assembling a brand around yourself the minute that you start conversing with others about your real estate property. You never know where these discussions are going to lead you - so monitor your image savagely. How about we look a bit more profound at how to adequately showcase your own particular individual brand?

Be Honest

As another real state specialist, you are not going to know everything and that is 100% all right. One of the snappiest approaches to ruin your reputation is the point at which you begin talking about things that you don't really know much about. When you attempt to put on a show of being a "specialist" and you're not one, other genuine real estate investment specialist will know instantly and they will not hide it from you. Concede what you don't know and utilize that to learn. Truth be told, one of the most ideal approaches to develop, as a businessperson is to solicit a great deal from inquiries and, in quietude, listen to the individuals who are willing to share their knowledge to you. Additionally, don't distort yourself. What you'll once see in a while is another speculator going ahead, the scene and presenting them in that capacity. At that point, in only a couple of days, they discuss having "properties in every one of the 50 expresses" that they are willing to offer on rebate. Unless that individual abruptly acquired many properties overnight, that individual is likely distorting themselves. As a rule, that individual is simply a wholesaler after the exhortation of a master some place and attempting to construct a purchasers list for their future arrangements. Yes, assembling a purchaser's rundown is unimaginably imperative.

You have to focus on your needs first and then evaluate the property. Don't be attracted to something at first site you have to look around quite a bit if you wish to zero in on the right type of property. Don't over rely on others and their opinions. Since you are going to buy the property, it will be entirely your choice and responsibility to pick the best option. If at any time you feel like you are not happy with your choice, you can look for another one and sell you old house.

You'll additionally discover new real estate investors showcasing arrangements by means of Craigslist or different locales, yet these are arrangements that they have no enthusiasm for. These individuals might lie about making arrangements to get different speculators who may be occupied with them. On the off chance that you get busted lying around an arrangement, guaranteed is that these people, who find it out, would not like to work with you anymore

Respectability

Do you do what you say you will do? Your respectability is the thing that will hold individuals returning to work with you, over a long period of time. As a real estate investor, your notoriety will go before you wherever you go. This implies that you have to consistently make certain you are acting with the most elevated amount of uprightness. Envision a moneylender who guarantees to loan yet he pulls out at last minute. Would they keep on growing their business? What about a real estate investor who undermines his customers and swoops in on all the great arrangements under his customers' feet? Would he keep on improving his image? Your trustworthiness is an indispensable piece of your image. Keep up the most elevated gauges of respectability and other people will discover and make business with you.

Polished Methodology

It is safe to say that you are anticipating maintaining a diversion or a business? On the off chance that you need to be seen as business proficient, you can begin at this moment. Each choice you make, each relationship you manufacture, and each thing you purchase: Be proficient. You don't need to be a million dollar business to resemble one. Appearing to a house with a filthy Hawaiian shirt and shorts likely isn't going to give you the expert picture you need to succeed. The same goes for the business cards you arrange, the voice message on your telephone, and the presence of your vehicle. Individuals trust experts - so begin acting like one.

Types of recreational and commercial estates

Recreational properties
Recreational properties, as the name suggests, are those that are used for recreational purposes. So they are places, which are generally regarded as holiday homes. Recreational houses are some of the most sought after in the world of real estate, as people will have the chance to diversify their investments. These properties are generally located in great locations such as hillside, along a riverbed etc.

When you wish to buy recreational property, there are certain steps that you need to follow, which are as follows.

<u>Location</u>
The very first thing to look at is the location of the property. As you know, you need to have a good location for your property as it is going to be used for the purpose of recreation. So whether you wish to set up a zoo or a holiday home, the location should be such that it is in a natural setting. Most people prefer to choose locations that are unique and picturesque. You too must look for a place that is on top of a hill or inside a forest reserve or has a river close by etc.

Activity

The activity that is around the area is also important. You have to see what is happening and whether you have any neighbors. In general, it will be a good thing to have neighbors, as you will get to know about the area better. Speak with them and find out about the place. Ask them about the facilities that are available in the area and the overall reputation there. You have to try and get a clear picture of everything before you decide to buy a property or make an investment.

Things provided

Many times, these places come with a few things like a tank or a well, a fence around the property etc. You have to check if all that is mentioned on paper is provided to you. If even a single thing is missing then you should ask the owner about the same and tell him or her to either have it fixed or reduce the cost. For this, you have to personally visit the site and inspect everything. If you want anything else to be added, then you can request the owner for the same.

Wild life

It is important for you to check out the wildlife in the area. If there are any dangerous animals, then you will have to get your security intensified. You must also account for pests and raccoons and ensure that they are all curtailed. But if you are interested in having a wild life reserve, then you must ensure that you do not disturb the eco system. Your animals will have to lead a normal life and for that, you have to take precautions and work as per the norms of the land.

Transport

Check out the transport facilities that are provided in the area. See if they are good enough for people to move about freely. It is important to look for transport facilities such as local trains and buses. You have to check it out for yourself by travelling and ensuring that everything is proper.

Resources

You have to check out the resources that are available in the land. These include water to drink, irrigation facility, the quality of air etc. All of these will matter once you start living in the area. If one of these is bad, then check if the quality can be improved upon. If not, then see if it is possible to find another plot similar to it and drop the idea of buying this particular plot.

Advantages:

There are many advantages to investing in recreational properties. One of the biggest advantage is the chance to make back the money that you have spent on acquiring the plot or property. If you wish to use it as a vacation home, then you will be extremely pleased with your investment.

Disadvantages:

The main disadvantage is the hassle of looking for the best location for your investment. You might not easily find it and will have to spend some time looking for the best property. Another disadvantage is the maintenance cost. You will have to spend a lot of time and effort in maintaining the property.

Commercial

Commercial properties as you read earlier deal with buildings that are let out to offices. Such types of investments are great choices for all those that have the capacity to make large investments. If you don't have the appetite for big risk then it is best to avoid such investments. Let us look at some of the types of commercial spaces.

Single space

The first type of commercial space is known as the single space. As the name suggests, here, you will only let out a single shop to an office. It might be an independent shop or also might be in a building. Where you wish to have it is your choice entirely. The price of such an establishment might not be too high. You have to look for a place that is located in an ideal spot. Don't make the mistake of choosing something because it looks good from the outside. You have to look at all the features that come with it and then make your choice.

Buildings

Buildings refer to entire office buildings that you can buy and rent out. All the spaces will belong to you and you can either give it to a single office or to a collection of offices. Whatever works best for you can be made an option.

Advantages:

The advantage of office buildings is the cost of maintenance. You don't have to spend too much time or put in too much effort in maintaining the building. If there are other offices there then they will contribute towards maintaining the building.

Another advantage is how quickly you will be able to make back the money that you would have invested in the property. You won't have to wait too long and can make the money back within a few months' time.

Disadvantages:

The main disadvantage of office buildings is the high prices. You will have to shell out quite a lot of money if you wish to invest in office buildings. The cost generally runs into hundreds or thousands of dollars and you have to have that kind of a budget if you wish to invest in office properties.

Another disadvantage is getting different offices to get along with each other. Each one will have a different policy and they will start bickering and fighting with each other.

If you are looking to invest in recreational or commercial properties then you must do ample research on the subject. Only after you have understood everything that there is to about them should you invest in them.

Chapter 7: Raising Finances For Your Real Estate Investments

When it comes to financing your house or project, there are many choices to choose from. We will look at all of these choices and see, which the best one for you is.

Bank loans

Bank loans are the most preferred mode of financing real estate. These loans are issued by nationalized and public banks and are available easily. All you have to do is fill up the forms and place a property or an asset as collateral to your borrowing. The collateral can be the new property itself. Sometimes, it helps to approach a bank through someone that you are well acquainted with. They will help you get the loan fast enough. But remember that banks will only give you 90% of the amount and the remainder has to be your personal money.

Credit unions

Credit unions are like banks. They will give money to the borrower at a discounted rate. These are like co-operative societies that give money to the borrowers at a discounted rate. But, you will have to be a member of the society. If you are not one, then you must approach someone who is a member there. You can easily save on a few hundred dollars if you opt for this financing method. If you are unable to track down any member, then try talking to them and ask them for a sum of money to be borrowed.

P2P

P2P is better known as peer-to-peer lending. As the name suggests, p2p refers to money being exchanged between friends. It is obvious that you will have friends who belong to all walks of life. You will have those that have the capacity to fund your business as well. You can ask them for the money and tell them that you will pay it back after a certain period of time. They might not charge you a high rate of interest like your bank would and so, it will be a good choice for you, especially if you are not capable of paying a big rate of interest. Sometimes, it might not be a single friend it might be a group of friends.

Finance companies

There are some finance companies that you can approach to fund your estate. These companies will give the investor money that they can invest in their business. All you have to do is tell them about your real estate investment and ask them to finance it. They will charge you a certain rate of interest that might be a little high or low as compared to bank loans and will entirely depend on the company's reputation. If you successfully pay back the money that you borrow, then their trust in you will increase and they will readily give you a loan for your next project.

Investors

Apart from finance companies, there are also individual investors that will fund your project. These investors will be looking for places where they can invest their money and earn a certain rate of interest on it. You can approach them and avail the loan from them. You must produce your credit report and show them that you are capable of returning the money to them. If your credit report is bad, then they might ask you for a higher rate of interest. You have to try and get any errors in your credit report fixed if you wish to lower the rate of interest that the individual will charge you.

Families

One option is for you to approach your family for the money. If you have any family members that are willing to pay you then they might not charge you a hefty amount for it. It need not be just one family member and you can approach two or three and ask them to fund your investment. If you already have a bank loan, then you can choose to borrow from your relatives and pay back the bank. That way, you will have the chance to save on quite a lot of the interest money that you owe to the bank.

Government

There might be a few government schemes available in your city, which help in funding your real estate business. They might not charge you an exorbitant rate of interest and will only be quite nominal. You have to look for these schemes and check if you are eligible for them. If you are not, then check if someone you know is. You can ask them to sign up and avail the benefits and pass it on to you. You can offer them a stake in the deal as a reward for their help.

Insurance

You can also contact an insurance company for the same. You would pay a certain amount to the company on a monthly basis and you can borrow a sum using that money as your collateral. They might charge you a fee for it but it will all work in your favor, as you will have the chance to return the money back into your insurance account. Once you do, you will have your investment on one hand and the insurance money on the other.

Foreign investors

Foreign investors are people that belong to your country but have settled elsewhere. They will be interested in investing their money in their country and looking for opportunities to do so. When you approach them, they will be interested in partnering with you, provided you give them a small share in the investment. That will be a good deal for you, as you will have the chance to get your investment funded and also partner with someone who will bring value to the deal. Just ensure that you have all the details of the contract mapped out before entering into the deal in order to avoid any discrepancies.

REITs

REITs stand for real estate investment trusts. These are like stocks and are listed on the stock market. When someone buys them, you will receive a funding for your investment. It is possible for you to receive a 100% funding through this method. But once the project is up, you will have to pay the individual investors a certain amount of money as a return on their investment. REITs are generally seen as a great way to source your finance, as they will greatly help in diversifying your finance options.

These form the different ways in which you can finance your real estate properties.

Some of the best places to look for property listings

Agents

You have to keep in touch with some of the agents in your area who will have access to all the best properties. They will be able to direct you towards the most ideal properties in your area. Your agents will alert you as soon as something comes up. You can then go and check out the property and buy it if you like it.

Clubs

You have to join clubs where people interested in properties meet on a regular basis. When you interact with people, it is obvious that you will come face to face with those that deal in properties on a regular basis, you are sure to stumble upon something that will suit your need. These clubs will be located all over town and you must look them up online or ask around about them. Attend the meetings from time to time and be on the lookout for the best properties in town.

Classifieds

It also pays to keep an eye on the classifieds. These can be both online and newspaper. Maybe you will find a good deal that will work well for you. Similarly, you should check newspaper classifieds from time to time. You might end up finding a rare distress sale property, which will work great, for you.

Auctions

You have to look for and attend auctions. Have a budget in mind and start bidding for a property of your choice. Don't make the mistake of going into an auction without a set budget in mind. You will end up over spending. Bid for houses that you think are really worth it and you will surely be rewarded for it.

Chapter 8: The Don'ts of Real Estate

There are quite a few don'ts when it comes to real estate investments and we will look at them in this chapter.

Don'ts of Real estate

Don't No.1 – confidence is key

Confidence is key when it comes to investing in real estate. You have to remain confident of your decisions and not think too much into it. If you like a property very much then there is no point not investing in it. You have to trust in your instinct to do all the right things and not worry too much about it. At the same time, you should try to not be over confident with your choice. You will end up making mistakes if you think you can never go wrong with your decisions. Remain confident and do the right thing.

Don't No.2 – overnight results

Do not make the mistake of expecting overnight results. Such a thing does not exist in this world and you will not see any overnight results. You will have to wait for at least a few years before any results come through. Maybe it will take you 5 years or maybe just 1 year, but you have to remain patient all through out if you wish to gain out of your investment. Many of the millionaire investors that exist in the world would have waited a few years before seeing any substantial result and you must do the same. But don't worry; once you get the ball rolling, everything will be fine.

Don't No.3 – Don't get the math wrong

Some people have the habit of being too casual with their math. They will think it is okay to simply add up the numbers roughly in their head and go ahead with the deal. That will cause you to be upset later as your budget will be over shot. So, you have to try and calculate as accurately as possible and not do mere mental calculations. Make sure you carry a small journal and a calculator everywhere that you go and calculate it immediately. Write all of it down and tally everything finally. See if it is within your budget and make changes if it is not.

Don't No.4 – Taxes

Being prepared for your taxes is the most important thing when you wish to invest in property. You have to be prepared to file for taxes and pay them on time. Don't think when the time comes you will easily be able to pay the taxes. That will not happen. You have to plan everything in advance and ensure that everything is in its place. Many people make the mistake of keeping their tax duties till the end. You will find it very difficult if you do so and so, it is a must that you plan all of it well in advance.

Don't No.5 – Don't keep things to yourself

Do not make the mistake of keeping information to yourself. You do not have to keep everything a secret. Share the information with others and speak to them about your real estate investments. Maybe you will share it with a well wisher and they will guide you through it.

These form the different don'ts that you must bear in mind while investing in properties.

Dos of real estate

Bargain well
It is extremely important for any real estate investor to bargain well. There is no point in straight away settling for what the owner is demanding from you. You have to argue and settle it a little bit. If you are not good at haggling then take along someone who is. That way, you will be able to get the property at a price that suits you well. If the owner is not at all interested in haggling then it is best that you decide to walk away from the deal altogether. If they feel like they are losing a good client then they will surely contact you again.

Indulge in flipping
Flipping is a great concept to use when you wish to make quick money out of your real estate investments. With flipping, all you have to do is buy a property, renovate it and then sell it for a higher price. This will take some time and some amount of mastery to fulfill. First, you have to scour for a good deal. Head out and look for good deals on houses. Haggle with the owner and have the price reduced. Once you buy the house, renovate it to the best of your ability. You have to make it likeable. Then, look for the next buyer and sell the house to them. You can keep flipping houses as much as you like.

The buy & hold strategy
There are many strategies that you can use to avail long term benefits from your real estate investments. One of these strategies is known as the buy and hold strategy. The buy and hold strategy is one where you buy the house and hold it. This means that you are looking for a good time to

dispose off your property. In the meantime, you can allow a relative to stay and take care of the property. That way, you will have the chance to sell the house at the right time to the right people. As soon as you think the price is right, you can dispose off the property. This is a better technique to employ as you will have ample time to work on your project and will not feel rushed. If with time you feel like holding on to the property then you can do so.

Hybrid deals

A hybrid deal is a combination of the previous two. You will have the option of either flipping the house immediately or buy and hold it for some time. You have to be sure as to what you want to do with the property. If you have enough resources to spend, then you can invest in two properties and subject each to a different treatment.

Sub-letting

Sub-letting is a concept where you rent a house and then rent it out to someone else. That way, you will be able to make a bit more money out of it. Say for example you are renting a place for $500. You can then sublet it for $100 and that will be your profit. But you have to make sure that the owner is okay with you subletting the property. You don't want to get into trouble for it later.

These form the different dos of real estate and you will have the chance to make the most of your investments by following these.

Chapter 9: Basic Criteria to Consider While Buying Property

Here are some of the important criteria to consider when you wish to invest your money in real estate properties.

Location of the property

When it comes to choosing your property, there are a few things that you must bear in mind. Property buying is no child's play and only those that think long and hard will be able to buy lucrative property. For that, it is important to take the right steps and ensure that you do it correctly right from the very beginning. The different steps are explained as follows.

Property size

The very first thing to look into is the size of the property. It is important to check the size from end to end. You can carry a measuring tape with you if you like and ensure that you are getting exactly how much you were promised. You can also get a friend or partner to help you out, as the area will be quite large. Remember that estimates don't work when it comes to property. You have to have the exact numbers. In general, the bigger the plot the, better the deal. Regardless of whether you are looking to build a small house or a big one, it is best for you to look for a plot that is big enough. One idea is to look for a big property no matter what will go on it. After your building has been set up, you will have enough space around it to construct another building or add in another feature. You can also easily expand your existing building if there is enough space around it. Remember that around 20% of the area around your building will be utilized for common space and you have to bear that in mind before buying a property.

Price of the property

The next important criterion is to look at the price of the property. As you know, you will have to work as per a budget. If the price is too high, then you must haggle as much as possible. But that is only if you like the property. Before that, you should look for prices that are to your liking. Start with properties that are priced at least 10% lesser than your budget. That will ensure that you stay within your budget and will be prepared for any extra costs that might crop up later. Do not make the mistake of looking for a property without having a budget in mind. You will end up over spending. You will also not have a clear idea of what the value of the plot is. Conduct ample research before you go ahead with the deal. Ask around and see if you are being quoted the right price for your property. It is better to pay the price in bulk rather than in installments. This is especially true if you are taking up a loan for the project.

Location

The location of your property is also quite important. You have to find one that is in an area of your liking. There should be ideal resources present all around. The ideal resources depend on what you plan to do with your property. If you wish to make it a wildlife reserve then you will have to look for a forest and wildlife around you. If you are buying it for a residential purpose then markets and transport facilities should be located nearby. Similarly, you must look for the best possible location for your property if you wish to remain satisfied with your buy for long. Everybody has a dream location in mind and you too should have one. Make an exhaustive list of all the different features that you will want in your property. When you visit the site, see if at least 90% of the items on the list are available. If they are not, then it is best to move to another plot. The same extends for a house. Look for a majority of the criteria and settle for it only if you are thoroughly satisfied with the location.

What comes with the property

As a property buyer, you have to understand that certain things always come with properties. You have to find out what is being provided with yours. It can include fittings, furniture's, appliances etc. Sometimes, it will be extremely important to get these. So, you will have to go to the site yourself and inspect it. If you find that any of the promised items are missing, then you have to speak to the owner and ask for them to be provided to you. Many people count normal things like bulbs and fans to be necessities and if the owner is charging you for these then you must first ensure their presence and also see if they are working fine. One important aspect to heck for a commercial property is the availability of parking space. You will obviously need a large parking space for a building. See to it that you are provided with a covered space and not an open one. Underground storage units are also important and should be included with your property. Check everything out before buying the property and also have it cleaned before buying it. If there are any electrical issues then that too should be corrected.

Fencing the property

Many people make the mistake of putting up just a signboard calling the land theirs. That is not enough and fencing is a must. Whether it is a plot of land meant for residential purposes or to create a commercial building, you have to get it fenced. Fencing will help you know your limits. You have to invest in a strong fencing system and can have professionals come and install it. If another person's fence is encroaching your land, then you should call them up and ask them to move the fence from your land. Many times, people get confused with their own site and don't understand which one is theirs and which one belongs to their neighbor. In such a case, you can take along a surveyor or a site engineer and ask him to identify the site for you. Once you find out which one is yours, you can have a fence placed all around it. If you find that someone has encroached, you can ask the engineer for advice.

Steps of buying the property

Once all the previous steps have been taken care of, you have to move to the process of buying the property. As you know, it is not really easy to buy property. There are a million things to take care of and each and every minute detail needs to be taken care of. The very first step of this process is to negotiate for the property as much as possible. You obviously do not want to pay the owner whatever price he is asking for. You have to go in with confidence and negotiate for the plot as much as possible. You have to understand the different skills that are required for the same and not appear confused. You should know exactly what you want out of it and be completely aware of how much you can actually spend. Once that is done, you have to contact your lawyer. Your lawyer will look at the property papers that have been supplied to you and crosscheck its veracity.

Raising finances

The next step is to raise enough finances to make the payment. Remember that you will not be required to pay the full money at once and can do so in installments. Once you make the initial payment, you will have time to make arrangement for the remainder. For that, you will have to approach a bank or any of the other institutions that were mentioned. It is important that you approach a place that is giving you a good rate of interest. For that, you have to do some research. Even before that, you have to get your credit scores checked. See if you have any bad credit. That has to be rectified first and only then will your loan be approved. If you have a bad credit score then you have to send it for correction. First apply for your credit scorecard from one of the 3 credit agencies. Then, check if everything is correct on the card including your name and address. If it is not, then you have to send it for correction. Next, check for any erroneous entries on the card. This will seem impossible but it is a possibility. Maybe the creditor has made two entries or there is a similar problem. Once that is rectified, your credit score will improve and you will avail loans at a good rate of interest.

What the future holds

When you buy a property, you must always evaluate it from a future perspective. You have to understand how much it will be valued at in say 10 years' time. Will it fetch you more money? Will it be valued lesser? To know the answers to these questions, you must ask around and seek the answers. Remember that you will not get answers to these easily and will have to ask the right people. You can ask the surveyor at least and find out what the prices were like a few years before. That will give you a good idea of what your land will be valued at after a few years. You can utilize the classic idea of buying a property in an upcoming area. That way, you will have the chance to capitalize upon its popularity. Pick a good and upcoming locality to begin with. Do your research and personally look at all the localities. Don't rely on only opinions. You must do your own research when it comes to buying properties of your choice.

Evaluating your buy

It is obvious that you will have quite a lot of expectations out of your property investments. Once everything is done, you have to literally measure your satisfaction. You have to check whether the property has hit all the ticks in your list. Apart from personal satisfaction, you also must measure the asset value. It should steadily rise in value and over a period of time, you have to receive a higher value for the property. You have to calculate the value by looking into the current prices and arrive at an amount, which will be its actual value in a few years' time.

Chapter 10: Mistakes to Avoid in Real Estate

There are a few mistakes that you must avoid while making property investments and they are as follows.

Impatience

It is important to be as patient as possible when making real estate investments. Do not make the mistake of rushing into something, as it will come undone. Take your time and do as much research on the topic as possible. Once you find the property, look into each and every detail of it. If you miss out on small things then you will lose sight of the bigger picture. It is better to be safe than sorry and so; it is best that you remain as patient and diligent as possible while looking for real estate properties. Don't be disheartened even if it takes a very long time for you to find the property of your choice. As long as you keep the search going you will have the chance to find the best property in the world.

No research

Many people make the mistake of looking for houses that are located far off. They will rely on online ads to look for places that are located away from where they currently reside. That, however, is a big mistake. You must look at houses in your neighborhood as it will be easy for you to search and you might find a lucrative deal. Just head out and look for properties in and around where you are put up. You can hire an agent if you like and look for houses that are within your budget. There are many online sites that list properties and you can type in your budget and find houses that fit your criteria.

No budget

A budget is the most important tool that you have to use when you are thinking of investing in properties. Not only should you use it while buying property but also while auctioning for one. Don't go into an auction with an unlimited budget. You will end up over spending. You have to have a limited budget and not overspend. You will tend to get carried away at these auctions and it is vital that you bear in mind the exact amount that you will be willing to pay towards the property.

Marketing

When it comes to selling your old house, you have to market it as efficiently as possible. Do not make the mistake of relying on traditional methods and use the Internet as much as possible. You have to market your house in such a way that the buyer is instantly attracted to it and will be glad to buy it from you. Even if there are flaws, you have to mask it in the best possible way. But it is best to address all the issues as soon as possible and ensure that the house is in a movable state.

Site visit

Never make the mistake of buying a property without a site visit. You will not know how the site looks and what the features are. You don't want to risk buying a property that is not well maintained. Many people think that looking at the pictures of the property is enough and they will get a clear picture of how it looks. But you have to understand that people make use of special angles and high-resolution cameras that take high definition pictures and make the site look extremely big and nice. You will be fooled if you think you will get what you see in pictures.

Remodeling before selling

There is a difference between touching up and remodeling. Do not make the mistake of remodeling or renovating your house before selling it. You can touch it up if you like to make it a bit more presentable but don't make the mistake of putting in heavy installations. You will end up regretting it as it will add to your costs and the people buying it might not like it and have it demolished. So don't think for your customers and allow them to change the house to their liking.

Hidden charges

Whether you are looking to buy a plot of land or an entire house, you have to be prepared to bear certain hidden costs. These costs will not be apparent and the owner might not mention them expressly to you. You have to ask him about these costs and add it to your expenses. It is important to avoid any miscalculations, as that will throw your budget off. Remain as strict as possible when it comes to your budget and avoid extending your hand as much as possible.

Wants and needs

You have to understand the difference between wants and needs when it comes to investing in real estate. When you plan to accumulate on properties for personal collection and long-term investments then you must buy what you want and not want you need. On the other hand, if you plan to sell it and buy another property in succession then you must buy what you need and not what you want. You can manage with what you have when you plan to move out within a couple of years. The focus will be on how much you can profit from it.

These form some of the mistakes that you must avoid when you invest in real estate. Remember that you have to avoid these under all circumstances and not end up making a mistake. You will regret it and feel awful for having known about it and yet committing it.

Chapter 11: FAQs on Real Estate

When we take up a new topic, it is obvious that we will have a few doubts on the subject. In this chapter, we will look at the different questions that get asked on the topic and answer them one by one to help you have a clear understanding of the subject.

Are real estate investments lucrative choices?

Yes. Real estate investments are great choices to make. You will have the chance to double or even triple your income just by buying a house or property. Many people are apprehensive when it comes to real estate investments, as they fear having to deal with loses. But loss and gain are part of any investment and you have to be prepared for anything. If you take the right steps and go about it in an orderly fashion then you will surely be able to make the most of your property and real estate investments.

Will I avail tax benefits?

Yes. You can avail a lot of tax benefits from your real estate investments. All you have to do is understand the taxation policy and you will be able to save on quite a bit of money. You can avail two types of tax benefits when you invest in property. One will be when you are selling your house and the other will be when you are buying a house. Both times you will have the chance to get away with some tax exemptions. You can also file joint returns with a partner and avail a further discount. Once you get the hang of it, you will understand how all of it is done.

Can I make it a career choice?

Yes. You can turn it into a career choice if you like. You have to take it up seriously and see to it that you are able to balance your current job and do part time real estate. Then, when your real estate business picks up traction, you can quit your job and take it up full time. Many people have availed great benefits by taking it up full time and you too can have the same, provided you do all the right things.

When is the best time to start?

There is no good or bad time to start investing in real estate. You have to start early if you wish to make the most of it. Anybody over the age of 18 can invest in real estate if they have the resources to do so. Even minors can if they have a guardian looking into their financial affairs. Once you understand how lucrative real estate really is, there is no point in wasting anymore time. You should get started at the earliest and ensure that you are taking all the right steps towards establishing your career in real estate investments.

Can I accumulate properties?

Yes. You can accumulate properties if you like. All it takes is a little patience and you will see that you are able to amass many properties. But don't have unreasonable expectations. It will obviously take a little time before you are able to collect such properties. You have to have a 15 or 20 year plan and work accordingly. Many people prefer to not accumulate properties and dispose them off as soon as they arrive at a lucrative deal. You too can do the same but must ensure that you are disposing it off at the right time.

Can I transfer properties?

Yes. You can transfer your property to whoever you think is fit to be awarded. It need not always be your children or spouse and can be any relative. Don't hesitate in writing down who will get what property and when. In fact, if you now own a lot of properties then it is extremely important that you prepare official papers and ensure that everything is well sorted out. You don't want to end up in trouble later or have discrepancies hounding you. Get hold of a good lawyer and have all your papers sorted out.

Are family properties investments?

Yes. Family properties or those that you have inherited are investments. They will grow in value over a period of time and that makes it an investment. Regardless of whether you are the sole owner or have to share it with siblings, it will prove to be an investment choice. You have to pursue it as an investment and ensure that all the papers in regard to it are safe.

Will it be part of my portfolio?

Yes. Real estate investments are part of your portfolio. You can list them along with the stocks and bonds that you own. Your real estate investments are meant to be your long-term investments and something that you will hold on to for a minimum of 2 years.

What are REITs?

REITs stand for real estate investment trusts and are part of the stock market. They are listed just like regular stocks and are traded on a day-to-day basis. You have to understand that these will be part of your stock investments and not real estate investments. But the two are connected. You can buy them at a low price and then avail monthly dividends. If they happen to rise in price then you can quickly dispose them off and avail a profit.

Can I go global?

Yes. You can invest in global properties. There are certain countries laws that you need to bear in mind and if you remain within them then you will be able to make foreign investments. You can also invest in foreign REITs and diversify your stock portfolio. Take the help of a good stockbroker to start investing in these REITs.

These form the different FAQs on the topic and I hope you had yours answered efficiently.

Chapter 12: How to Make Tax Free Money

When it comes to buying and selling property, there is one thing that most people worry about—taxes. It is obvious that you will have to pay taxes when you buy and sell houses but you have to make the right choices and ensure that you have enough

Selling

The very first step of the process is to sell your existing house. The sales proceeds from your existing house is what will fuel your next purchase. So start by looking for people who are genuinely interested in buying your house at the price that you are quoting. You have to try to fix a price that is just as much as the highest priced house in the locality. That way, people will be interested in seeing your house and will approach you. If you price it low to start with, then people will haggle and try to reduce it as much as possible. That is not something you want for your house. The criteria to sell your house is that you have to own it for 2 years or have lived in it for 2 out of the last 5 years. The latter refers to a situation where you might have rented it for 2 years and then bought it in the third year. *As per the* IRS, *you have the chance to be exempt from tax to the limit of $250,000.*

Buying new one

The next step is to buy the new house. The new house has to be one that is much cheaper than what you sold the old house for. So, you will have to perform a fair amount of research before buying. Also, you have to buy one that is priced much lesser than other houses in its price bracket. That way, you get to save on a lot of money. Start looking for houses that are valued at a price that is within your budget. For that, you will have to do some extensive research. Apart from looking at online sources, you must also contact agents. Tell them your budget and ask them to look for houses in the same price range. You must also keep the search going and ensure that you find a house in the right price range. If you find a house that is priced in and around the price you are looking for, then you must haggle and buy the house. We had earlier looked at the point, which said that you must not get emotionally attached to a house. The same extends here and look for a house that is nice and meets at least 50% of your expectations.

Timing your purchase

It is extremely important that you buy your house within the first few months of the year. You must not allow it to go into the later months, especially year-end. If you get this step wrong, then you will end up paying unnecessary taxes. It is best that you start looking at least 6 months in advance, which will make it September and October in case you wish to buy the house in March. So start the hunt in advance. It is okay if you are unable to find the house within that time. If you do find it in October, you must enquire if you can buy it in January. If that is not possible, then you should be ready to pay a little extra tax, which might eat away into your profit. Here, you must time your sale and buy within a few months. All this will seem like a daunting task the first time that you do it but with experience, you will know what to do when and be surprised at what you can actually achieve.

Manage

Many times, people are unable to time their buying and selling processes. They end up selling their house early and don't have another house to move into. In such a case, you can rent a place for the transitory time and look for another house to buy. Don't look for anything posh, just a simple house will suffice. Don't rush the process though. Look thoroughly and look for the best. If possible, you can also stay at a friend's place by paying a little rent. Just ensure that you don't overstay and keep your search on. Again, this process will get easier with time. You will know when to vacate a house and find a new one. If you have the chance to move into another house of your own during the transit time then that will be the best option to pick. You won't have to worry about paying a rent and will have an easy mind to look for another house.

Saving money

This is easily the best step of the process. You will have the chance to save on money that you make from your transactions. Now say for example you sell your old house for $800,000 and look for another one for $600,000. The difference of $200,000 is your tax-free profit. Isn't that simply wonderful? You will have the chance to make that kind of money every two years! Provided you do all the right things. Once you start doing it, the habit will start settling in and you will see how everything works in your favor.

Filing taxes

When you are ready to file your taxes, you have to fill out all the forms correctly. If you need help with it then avail services of a surveyor. One thing to understand here is that you can file joint returns with your partner and double your exemption by doing so. So, you have the chance to remain with $500,000 without having to pay any taxes. So, it is best that you and your partner file joint returns and save on a majority of the money that you remain with as profit from your home's sales proceeds.

Repeat

With time, you will be able to buy new houses and sell them off with ease. You will understand the tricks of the trade and also know how best you can minimize on the losses. Once you start selling and buying houses and then selling and buying again, you will be able to establish a loop and things will start falling into place automatically. You will have to remain keen on doing it for a long time and ensure that you are repeating the steps in the correct order.

Dedication

Remember that it will require a lot of dedication from both you and your family members as it will not be easy selling and buying new houses. You have to have the right spirit and welcome the challenge with open arms. Again I reiterate, it will get easier as you go and will not have to put in as much effort as you would at the beginning.

These form the different steps that you must adopt when you wish to buy and sell houses in loop and remain with a profit.

Chapter 13: Investing in Foreign Properties

Investing in foreign properties is no cakewalk. There will be a million things to look into and it is extremely important for you to take all the right steps. In this segment, we will look at the different steps in detail.

Hunting

The very first step of the process is to hunt for the right place. You will have to put in just as much effort as you would while looking for a house in your local country. You will have to find the property, do a personal visit, look for good deals etc. If you are unable to visit the site yourself and live in another country then you can employ someone to look into the properties in the other country. It can be a relative or an agent that you have employed. Ask them to send you genuine pictures of the property. Once everything is settled, it is best for you to visit the site yourself and look at the plot of land.

Laws of the land

Next, understand all the laws of the land. You have to understand everything that there is to know about investing in properties located in the foreign country. You don't want to make a mistake and ensure that you have understood everything that there is to. You can hire a surveyor or a valuator and ask them everything that there is to know about properties. If you are unable to find any information at all, then it is best to ask the locals about it.

Finance

The next step is to finance your investment. You have to look for places that will give you a loan for your investment. Remember that it will not be as easy as getting a loan in your local country. You will have to put in a lot more effort for your loan to be approved for your foreign investment. They will ask you for some valuable collateral and your credit score will be scrutinized. You have to be prepared for all of that and ensure that everything goes smoothly for you.

Buying

The next step of the process is buying the house. In order to buy the house, you will have to get your lawyer involved. You have to give him the papers and ask him to peruse it. If it is in a foreign language then you should ask the owner for an English document. Once you receive it you can have your lawyer go through it for you. If he finds something suspicious in it then you should clarify it with the owner. Once everything is settled, you can buy the property.

Renting

You can rent the place out to someone or have a relative occupy the house until such time as you can move in. You must try to price the house competitively and not exercise leniency. After all, you need to make back the money that you have spent on the property.

Taxes

The same rent taxes that apply in your local country extend to your foreign properties. You have to understand the taxation policies thoroughly before renting or leasing out the property.

One word of advice is to invest in a country whose currency value is much lower as compared to the value of your local currency. You will have the chance to buy a big house and can earn quite a handsome sum from your investment.

Chapter 14: Taking Care of Property

If you have a lot of property then it is extremely important for you to take good care of it and also ensure that the right people get it from you. In this segment, we will look at the different things that you must do to safeguard your high profile property.

Estate planner

The first step is to look for an estate planner for your properties. Start with the Internet and look for the best one. It is also a good idea to approach a bank to help you find a good planner. Once you are awarded an estate planner, you must lay out all the papers in front of him or her. You must be as honest as possible and for that reason you have to find a trustworthy valuator.

Valuation

The next step is to allow the valuator to value your property. He or she will do a personal inspection of all your properties and value them one by one. They will do so keeping in mind the current rates. Once all your properties have been valued, he will hand out a conclusive list with all the values tallied with the properties.

Drafting

The next step is to draft the final draft that will carry information about which property should be handed out to whom. You have to work closely with your lawyer. If you have children, then it is best to have them in the room when you wish to draft the property allotment. This step need not necessarily be a will and can only be an official property allotment meeting.

Finalize

Once the previous step is done, you must finalize the draft and ensure that everything in it is proper. If you want to make any amends then do so immediately.

These form the different steps that you must undertake when you wish to evaluate your property and hand it out to the appropriate people in your family.

Chapter 15: Container Homes

The newest entrant in the world of real estate is container homes. Container homes are exactly what they mean, homes that are made out of containers. These containers are cargo containers that are used to transport heavy equipment. They are available by docks. There is a step-by-step procedure that you have to follow in order to invest in container homes and they are as follows.

Land

When you plan to buy a container home, you might not find one that is readymade. You will have to do all the planning yourself and build a container home from scratch. Since it is a container home and not a fancy villa, it will be a good idea to choose a posh location for it. Your location can be by the river or in a forest. You will feel at peace for having chosen a calm and serene atmosphere.

Plan

Next, you must plan your container home. Choose a feasible plan, which is practical. Start by choosing the type of model example single room, two room, four rooms etc. Then draw it out and ensure that you have a practical plan to work with. If you need inspiration then you can look up online. You will find a blue print of a model container home. You can make use of the same and add in a few personal touches to it. If you have an engineer or architect friend then you can consult him and come up with a plan for your container home.

Price

The next thing to decide upon is the budget. An average container can cost you around $3,500. But if you want something sturdy and lasting then you might have to pick one from the $5,000 range. Apart from the container, you will also have to buy some paint and decorations, which also should be accounted for in the budget. Ideally, you should set aside around $10,000 to $15,000 for your container home. If you have any spare money left at the end of it then well and good. But it is best to have a little spare money set aside for your project.

Container

The next step is to buy the container. The container can be bought from a dock. You must look up online and find one. There, you will have two choices. The first choice will be to settle for a container that has been abandoned by the company. You will have to carry it back and have it fixed before using it. The other option is to buy a container that is sold by a container company. They would have polished it and repaired it. These will cost you slightly more than the former but will be a better bet, as you will not have to do anything to it in terms of repairing it. Be sure to carry a sturdy vehicle that is capable of carrying or pulling a big cargo container.

Customization

It is possible for you to get the containers customized. If you want another window or door then you can ask the seller to do it for you. They might charge you a little extra for it but if it is to your taste then it is best to get it done. You can also have it custom painted or have some graphics done on the side. All of it will make your container look unique. If the seller is refusing to do it then you can carry it back and get someone else to do it for you. If you are able to do it yourself then well and good and can customize it to suit your taste.

Assembly

The next step is to assemble the container home. Choose the place where you would like to place the container. If you want to fix it then you will have to get a metal worker to weld long nails and force it into the ground. If you have more than one container, then place them next to each other as per your plan. You can improvise on the plan if you like and place the containers in such a way that look appealing and aesthetic.

Decoration

The next step is to do the interiors of the container. You can decorate it in any, which way you like. It is best to buy furniture that will fit inside the house. Look up online for furniture that is meant for container homes. Plan out the interiors of the container just as you would plan the exteriors. Try to keep it simple and according to your taste. You must also ensure that everything is safe and you have fenced the area.

Renovation

There is always scope for renovation. You can renovate the house by placing the containers on top of each other. You can make it a duplex or even a triplex house. Just make sure that your neighbors don't have an objection to it and you have due permission for your expansion plans.

You don't have to make the container home your full time home. It can also be a recreational home. If you don't plan to stay in it then you can rent it out. But you will have to look into the safety features of the place and ideally fence it to prevent miscreants from encroaching your property.

These are the different steps that you need to adopt when you wish to invest in container homes.

Chapter 16: Types of Homes to Buy

It is obvious that there will be many types of deals that will be available in the market when you wish to buy a property. In this chapter, we will look at the types of deals that you must go after, if you wish to make the most of your investment.

Hurried sales

A hurried sale or a distress sale is one where the person selling the property will be in a hurry to vacate it. Many reasons can contribute to such sales including a shit of residence, an urgent need for money etc. Such deals will be great choices for any investor, as you will get a good deal for a low price. But these deals will be extremely hard to come by and you have to scour for them and have to pursue them effortlessly as many people will be after them. Most of these deals will not be advertised in a big way. They will be mentioned in a newspaper or something that elusive. So you have to look for them extensively if you wish to find them.

In Bad shape

The next type of house to look for is those that are in bad shape. Bad shape can have many meanings. It can mean bad shape such that it needs to be razed to the ground and rebuilt or bad shape in the sense it requires renovation. You have to look for houses that fall into the latter category. The house should be such that it requires a little renovation but not too much. You can buy the house, pay for the renovations and then claim tax benefits for it. But the renovations should not be only about changing the paint or fixing a broken window. It has to be a bit more like changing the pipe system and roofing.

Foreclosed homes

You must be well aware of foreclosures. Foreclosures are those homes that are being auctioned away. They will be auctioned because the owner would have defaulted making a payment for the house. Foreclosed homes are easy to come by and you have to take part in property auctions. You have to bid for the house and make sure that you are bidding the right amount. If you feel like you are over bidding then take a back seat. Don't worry if you lose out on a property, another one is sure to come by. Once you get possession of the house, you must make the house officially yours.

FSBOs

FSBO's refer to properties that are advertised by the owners themselves. There will be no middleman or intermediary and you can directly buy it from the owner. What this will do is, help you avoid paying any agent's fees. The fees can sometimes be quite exorbitant and you will have the chance to avoid it. It is also possible for you to talk it out with the owner and reduce the price of the property as much as possible. All of this will go a long way in helping you save on quite a lot of money. If you are not interested in moving to the house yourself then you can decide to flip it. You buy it, renovate it and then sell it for a good price.

REIAs

You can buy houses that are referred by real estate investors association. These will provide you houses at nominal prices and good deals. But you have to regularly attend meetings in order to find the best property. If you happen to know someone who is a member of such an association, then you can ask them to help you out and refer you to a good property.

Family owned properties

Family owned properties are those that are owned by your own families. Maybe you don't stand to get the house but you can buy it from them for a price. Maybe they will be willing to give it to you for a reduced price. You have to ask them nicely and ensure that you draw up a foolproof plan. Even if the property needs to be renovated, you must bid for it. You will feel at peace knowing that a family property has been kept within the family.

Properties abroad

Foreign investments are also a great choice to make. You will have the chance to diversify your investments. Foreign properties are not easy to buy and you will have to put in a little effort. You must employ someone in the foreign country to be on the lookout for ideal properties. Once they do find it, you must ask them to send you pictures and it is best that you personally visit the site to look at the surroundings and all the resources that lie around it. Before you finalize the property, you have to check the taxation laws once again and ensure that double taxation does not set you back too much.

These form the different types of properties that you can invest in if you wish to get a good deal. But you have to look for them carefully as they will not readily be available to you. If you happen to find a property that is ideal then you must tirelessly pursue it. If you think many others are after the same property then do your best to out bid them. But don't worry if you don't get it, there is no point in getting disappointed as you will surely find another property that will be much better than the one you lost out on.

Chapter 17: Property Issues to Be Wary Of

Issues with local properties

Calculating Depreciation

Depreciation is one of the most dreaded of issues that worry homeowners. It is obvious that any property will depreciate over a period of time. It is important that you account for depreciation when you wish to sell a property. All properties depreciate over a period of 6 months and will keep depreciating. So, you have to account for it and lessen he value when you are expecting to sell the property. The IRS states that you have to calculate your depreciation over a period of 27.5 years. You have to take the help of someone who is aware of taxation policies to understand how you will be taxed. Now let us suppose you have a house that is worth $300,000. After 5 years, it will depreciate by 10%. So, you have to calculate it based on this depreciated value. You will have to minus it and make it $30,000 less for the property and then calculate your profit after the sale of the property. It is important that you know exactly how much money needs to be subtracted. Once you decide to sell the house, you should subtract it from your profit.

Emergencies

As you know, you will have to vacate your house after 2 years and for that, you should be fully prepared. But in case an emergency crops up and you have to vacate it within a year, then you should have a backup plan in place. Now let us assume, you plan to pay off debts and vacate your house in 5 years' time. Along the way, a family emergency forces you to sell the house. In that situation, you might have to lose out on a profit. So, you must have a backup plan in place if you wish to not end up losing on your investment.

Getting attached

Many people suffer from the problem of being too attached to a property. People tend to get over attached and don't have the heart to let go of the property. This can be a very big problem. Even if we make up our minds to not get attached, we end up not wanting to leave a place and hold on to the property. For this purpose, it is important that people not get over attached to a property. Try to think of it as just an investment like stocks or bonds.

Family issues

Many times, family problems might come by, which will be unforeseen. These can be personal problems such as divorces, separation etc. All these might force you to sell your property before its due time. So, it is important that you account for such emergencies and ensure that you have a backup plan in place. These family problems always come unannounced and if you are not prepared for them then you will be in trouble. So, try to remain as prepared for all of these as possible and ensure that you are taking the right steps towards it.

Timing

Timing can pose a problem when you wish to dispose off a property. Maybe you pick a time that is not good for disposing off the property. Even waiting for a few more days might help you get a good price for it. So, you have to know when exactly is the best time for you to dispose off your property and ensure that you are not taking impulsive decisions. Don't consult too many people at the time of disposal and stick with your gut instinct.

Issues with foreign properties

As you know, your problems will not be limited only to your local investments and will also extend to your foreign investments. In this segment, we will look at the difficulties that will crop up with your foreign properties.

Difficulties in buying and selling

It will not be easy for you to buy and sell property in a foreign country. You will obviously have to look for it well in advance and also employ someone in the foreign country to look out for the property. You will then have to travel back and forth for it, which can be quite tedious. Add to it the travel costs and ultimately, you will end up paying a lot of money for a property that you will not personally occupy. What's even worse is trying to sell that property. You will have to put in a lot of effort to do so. You have to find the right buyer, the right time to sell etc.

Difficulty maintaining

It will be extremely difficult to maintain your foreign property. You will not be able to go and check it from time to time. If you have rented it out then it will be even more difficult for you. If you wish to keep an eye on it then you will have to employ someone to do it for you. That will again cost you money. You will have a tough time if you wish to renovate or redo the house, as you will have to travel back and forth for it. You will also have to find someone who will be willing to redo a house in installments. Leaving them by themselves might cause them to mess things up, which will end up being another headache for you. So, it is important that you keep all of this in mind when you wish to buy a foreign property.

Family issues

Again, family issues might come up which will make it difficult for you to dispose off a property. If you have a joint property with a partner and they don't want to sell it then you will have difficulty in disposing it off. You will have to take their permission and if they don't agree then have to settle for a loss. Similarly, you might urgently need money and your only go might be to dispose off the house. You might have to settle for a loss and not get the amount that you were originally expecting to.

Double taxation

Double taxation is a bane for many people. If you buy a property abroad, chances are you will be taxed both in the foreign country and also in your home country. That can cause you to spend a lot of money. So, it is important that you check it out first and calculate how much exactly you will be charged. Being prepared is vital if you wish to avoid unnecessary charges later on.

These form the different issues that might crop up when you buy and sell properties in succession.

Key Highlights

When it comes to real estate, nothing but the best will do. So, it is important that you understand thoroughly everything that there is to about it and only then make your choice.

The first choice to make is the type of property to invest in. you have to choose between a commercial property, a residential property and a recreational property. All of these come with their fair share of pros and cons and it is entirely up to you to choose the best one for yourself.

There are many types of commercial properties and we had a look at them in detail. Similarly, there are many types of residential properties and there is nothing wrong in investing in both. The main idea is to diversify your investments and that is possible only if you buy many properties. These properties need not all be situated in the same place and can be scattered about. You can also buy foreign properties, as they will further enhance your portfolio.

Remember that it is important for you to raise enough finances for your investment. There are many sources of finance and we looked at each of them in detail. You can choose the one that will work best for you. That choice will depend on your credit report and how much interest you are willing to pay for the borrowed sum of money. If you pick a creditor, ensure that he is quoting a nominal interest rate. If they are charging exorbitantly then you must speak with them and ask them to reduce the price.

Real Estate

When it comes to taxation, there are many ways in which you can avoid it, especially when you buy or sell a new house. We looked at the things that you can do for it in detail and hope you take advantage of the information provided. Once you get the hang of it, you will realize that it is easy for you to do the needful. Many investors indulge in the activity and save on a lot of money.

If you wish to remain updated on the properties that are up for sale then you must become a member of an investors club. There, you will have access to properties that are in demand and be in a position to buy one of your choices. You have to keep looking out for ideal properties and will ultimately be rewarded with something great.

Never be in a hurry to buy any property. If you think a deal is too good to be true then it probably is. Maybe there is something that the owner is not telling you. You have to probe into each and every detail and see if the owner is providing you with all the information about the property. You have to visit the site yourself and ensure that everything is in place. If anything is wrong, then you must have it rectified. If that is not happening, then you must move away from it.

Remember that no deal is too good to let go off. If you think it is a wise decision to do so, then let go of it without thinking twice.

We looked at the types of houses that you should be on the lookout for when you buy properties. When you choose one of these, you will notice that you are able to save a lot of money and have also gotten a great house out of it. But it is obvious that these choices will not always be available and you will have to consciously look for them.

There are many issues that might crop up when you buy foreign properties. You have to know what they are and are wary of them. But don't panic, there is no need to worry about it. Once you identify them, you will see that it is easy for you to steer clear of them.

We also looked at the don'ts of property investments. Go through them once more if you like and ensure that you are able to avoid them.

It is important for you to have a business plan when you wish to start investing in properties. You will realize that it is important for you to have everything in place and working for you. We looked at the blueprint for the business plan and it is best that you go through it again if you wish to be fully prepared for it when you go ahead with your buying process.

We looked at the real estate investment management tactics. You have to firstly know what it stands for and why it is important for you to manage it in the best possible manner.

We looked at what container homes are and you can invest in them if you think they will help you diversify your portfolio. They will be easy to design and maintain. But before you adopt them, it will pay for you to do a little research and understand everything that goes into making these homes. Once you have a good blueprint, you have to approach a container seller and get a container for a good price. Assembling the home will be quite easy and you will not have to put in too much effort. It is also easy to expand the place as you can keep stacking these containers one above the other and create a duplex or triplex.

There are many mistakes that you must avoid when it comes to investing in real estate. We looked at some of the important ones and it is important that you look into all of it and avoid them at all costs.

Similarly, we also looked at the dos and don'ts of real estate and how you can steer clear of them. You must look at them again and ensure that you are doing all the right things towards your real estate investments.

Don't get too attached to any property, as you might not be able to sell it off on time. It is important to treat all property as just an investment and not a lifetime choice. If at any time you are in a great position to sell it off and make good money out of it then so be it. You have to instruct your family the same and tell them to not over attach themselves to a property.

We looked at how you can value your high profile property and distribute it amongst your family members. You must take it up seriously and get done with it as soon as possible.

As a last piece of advice, I would like to stress on the fact that you have to be as patient as possible when you wish to invest in real estate. You must also showcase patience if you wish to take it up as a career move. Don't rush into anything, as it will easily come undone. Go slow and make the most of your real estate investments.

Conclusion

Thank you again for purchasing this book!

I hope this book was able to help you to decide and prepare your own real estate investment journey. Real estate investment is not only financially fulfilling, it is also a great career move.

We looked at all the different aspects of real estate investments and how you can get started with it at the earliest.

The next step is to put everything into reality; amaze not only yourself but also everyone who will be able to know the journey you are taking. Be the star of everyone's lives by sharing everything you know as well. Who knows? Maybe you will be the next real estate investment mentor that your friend or one of your family members is looking for? You will be greatly appreciated!

Thank you and good luck!